James Ramsay

MONUMENTS TO A STOLEN REVOLUTION
& OTHER POEMS FROM BUCHAREST

Published in 2022 by
SMALL STATIONS PRESS
20 Dimitar Manov Street, 1408 Sofia, Bulgaria
You can order books and contact the publisher at
www.smallstations.com

ISBN 978-954-384-130-1

James Ramsay

MONUMENTS
TO A STOLEN REVOLUTION

OTHER POEMS
FROM BUCHAREST

Illustrated by Celia Ward

SMALL STATIONS PRESS

Contents

List of Illustrations

Celia Ward's black-and-white drawings are based on sketches and photographs from different regions of Romania

Introduction

These poems are verbal snapshots from when I lived in Bucharest, Romania, with my wife, Celia, and two young daughters, Sophia and Iona, between 2002 and 2005. They reflect random sights and experiences, some personal and domestic, others broader in scope. The background of many is the poverty still all too evident in Bucharest at that time, and the legacy of dictatorship visible in the contrast throughout the city between grandiose urban 'systematisation' and dilapidated remnants of old Bucharest, 'the Paris of the East'. Restaurants and cafés, churches and monasteries, markets, memorials, characters on the streets, neglected trees and pavements, stray dogs, clapped out taxis and the *metrou* with its performers and mendicants all are recorded from a personal angle, with no claim to objectivity.

My situation as Chaplain at the Anglican church in the centre of Bucharest was unusual. Part of an institution yet left to myself on the ground, I was neither entirely a professional nor entirely free-booting. My role took me into a wide range of situations – from homeless people's hostel to Patriarchal palace, prison to morgue, Embassy reception to street-children's feast, ex-pat business gathering to garret conversation with individuals still suffering from the Communist past. For normal reasons of pastoral confidentiality I could not write about many of these encounters. Yet they all helped inform my perceptions and understanding of what was around me.

Biserica Învierii, the Church of the Resurrection, is an English suburban-style red-brick building dating from 1914 (though dedicated only after the First World War), looking mildly exotic amid concrete apartment blocks next to the 'Garden of the Icon'. Its finances were precarious, and having constantly to dream up new fundraising ideas, at times I felt more impresario than priest.

Every month I also took a service for the small Anglican community in Sofia, the capital of Bulgaria. The two cities and two churches were very different. Bucharest lies in the Romanian Plain, close to a major earthquake faultline. Sofia is 1800 feet above sea level, surrounded by mountains. In Bucharest, with its own church building, I welcomed whoever came in off the street, of whatever nationality, destitute or super-rich, Western entrepreneurs, consultants and engineers, disinterested academics, shysters of every stripe... In Sofia church services were held in the basement of the Ambassador's residence, a building that communicated, from its emblazoned *porte-cochère* to its no-nonsense window entablatures, the prestige of imperial power – so only those with enough self-confidence to brave the security and perceived glamour of the venue joined our congregation. The basement itself was of course far from glamorous.

A number of poems are thus also about places and events in Bulgaria, or the short flight on a small shuttle plane which became my monthly commute. Other travel poems take in Budapest and Istanbul, as well as Transylvania and the Black Sea.

In 2002 the Romanian banking system was just beginning to stabilise, but everyday life was still a cash economy, with all the liveliness, unexpectedness, and precarity of a society with little regulation. Pavement stalls on Bulevardul Magheru sold lurid synthetic trinkets from the large Chinese trader community in the south of the city, while a few hundred yards away a designer coat could be bought at an inexplicably affordable price.

Romania and Bulgaria had applied for EU membership, and were soon to join NATO, yet corruption remained rife in politics, business, and the justice system. Living near the Spanish Embassy, we witnessed the queues for Spanish visas (considerably longer than those at the British Embassy) as people applied to go abroad for work. Widespread emigration and the ostentatious wealth of a few were different sides of the same coin. In the heat of summer, while air-conditioned limousines with tinted windows ferried the wealthy to their villas on Lake Snagov, women would stand at major intersections with bunches of sunflowers, ready to dart out into the traffic as soon as the lights turned red, to try to make a sale. Barely less dangerous than the windscreen-cleaning service offered by children at other lights.

Most people had limited access to healthcare, and herbal remedies were widely used. In the absence of large supermarkets people shopped for food in local markets and from informal pavement stalls. It was normal to see fruit and vegetables coming into the city in pick-ups or trailers or the backs of cars from individual properties and smallholdings. All shapes and delicious, they bore no resemblance to the camera-perfect yet all too often anaemic produce that came in as Western companies started to dominate.

Every two or three days a lady who owned six cows visited our block of flats with fresh milk in two-litre plastic mineral water bottles. The milk when decanted into a jug developed a thick crust of cream, delectable with honey from the local market. There was nevertheless far less obesity than in Britain, and April was indeed 'the cruellest month', when winter stores had run low and people were hungry. Many old people had insufficient pensions and were not uncommonly reduced to begging or offering a few eggs or herbs or family heirlooms to survive.

When we arrived in Bucharest, taxi fares were unnervingly cheap compared with other capital cities. Quite a number of drivers turned out to have degrees but could not find a professional job. The condition of some taxis was nothing short of an incentive to prayer – MOTs were not a legal requirement until about halfway through our time in Romania.

With Romanian Orthodox Christianity the majority religion, and religious observance and interest in theology part of mainstream life, visits to monasteries were popular rural outings. On the bus some people would cross themselves as we passed a church. Little children would rush on board trains in the underground, collapse to their knees by the support pole in the middle of the carriage, and rattle through the Lord's Prayer, or even the Nicene Creed, in time to take a collection before the next station.

Several poems are set in the *metrou*, with its cavernous marble-clad stations, snack kiosks, newspaper sellers, entertainers, and beggars, genuine and bogus. When shiny new carriages appeared on Line 1, they came with *paznici*, guards to keep out all such supposed low-life.

Impossible to ignore was the gigantic 'House of the People', the second largest administrative building in the world after the Pentagon, now home to the Romanian Parliament and the Museum of Modern Art (though most of the building remains unused). Intended as the crowning symbol of the Victory of Socialism under the Communist dictator Nicolae Ceaușescu, and his own personal palace, its construction drained the national coffers while throughout the country there was poverty and starvation. Swathes of the historic city centre were demolished to make way for it and the vast avenue leading up to it. It is rumoured that among the many who died during the process of construction were some monks who refused to leave their monastery as it was demolished.

Meanwhile dotted around the city are memorials to the revolution of 1989 in which Ceaușescu was overthrown. Of all the upheavals that saw the end of the Soviet era across Europe, the Romanian revolution was the only one in which the authorities responded by force, with inevitable bloodshed. After less than six months, however, disillusionment had set in. Apart from the removal of the dictator and his widely loathed wife, Elena, nothing seemed to have changed. Demonstrations against the interim government led to covert state-instigated violence resulting in many injuries and a number of deaths of protesters (the official death toll of six being challenged by reports of mass graves and over 128 dead). Some spoke of a 'coup' in '89 rather than a 'revolution'.

Those modest memorials, often with poignant inscriptions, were easy to miss in the bustle of everyday life as the revolution started to become history. I would pause and offer a prayer whenever I passed one. In stark contrast to the continuing corruption and lack of improvement in living conditions for most people, smart new memorials appeared for the fifteenth anniversary of the revolution in 2004.

Huge abandoned construction sites remained around the city, more or less as they were when work had been brought to an abrupt stop by the revolution. Large properties stood empty with security fences around them as pre-Communist ownership was legally established, the buildings becoming more derelict, the gardens more of a wasteland. Despite preservation orders, attractive nineteenth- and early twentieth-century French-style villas with vine-covered courtyards that had somehow survived the devastation of Ceauşescu's grandiose urban systematisation were fast being demolished by capitalist property developers.

The patronising and ill-informed way some in business and diplomatic circles talked about Eastern Europe, and their disregard for the cultural wealth of regional history and traditions made me cynical about Western claims to be helping Romania and Bulgaria 'transition' to new prosperity in a global market economy. As the ambassadorial residence in Sofia epitomised, empire and the long shadow of Great Power politics were historic realities with still powerful leverage. Adapting worship to our basement room there, and encountering destitution on the church doorstep in

Bucharest, I became more aware both symbolically and literally of the underside of power.

Much has changed in the years since we were in Romania. And much has not changed. The Covid pandemic has mercilessly exposed the realities of inequality, both global and within individual countries, especially countries like Romania where corruption still has a crippling impact on national wellbeing and the lives of ordinary citizens. In the UK too the pandemic has spotlighted wealth inequalities, infrastructure weaknesses, and high level shenanigans that were easier to ignore under 'normal' conditions. In other words, for all the differences in extent and degree of the difficulties in Romania, Britain has serious problems that in many respects are fundamentally very similar.

These poems, from a personal perspective at a certain moment in time, are offered in gratitude and respect for those who against great odds joy in life, and who defy disheartenment to inspire hope and joy in others.

DO NOT INSULT THE GOD

You see now what you should have seen before.
Euripides, *Bacchae*, l. 924 (tr. Robin Robertson)

Ice this morning
changed puddles
to burn scars.

A bunch of still unripe
grapes lies frozen
like the skin of a reptile
on the pavement.

Black vine leaves
and tendrils –
bacchic fuel
on balcony and window grilles
wrought a century ago or more –
have been re-glossed.

A few numbers along
the sleekly appointed EU
building opened last year

must prove
its vintage
in the frenzy

and awaking.

THE SAVOUR OF SALT

Matthew 5.13

The taxi driver gestures
to the beads swinging
from his windscreen mirror.
A bead taps
against his fingernail.

The vehicle smells of diesel,
hair oil, deodorizer,
and incense.

'These beads...'

For Bucharest
the driving is cautious.

Dancing to the vehicle's
movement, the moonstones
gleam as if lit from within.
'You suppose they're
plastic? They're tears

of

the Mother of God.'

Salt for shot shock absorbers
and outrageously low
fares.

'I find them...
beautiful.'

Disdaining my diplomacy
with a jut of his chin,

he focuses
on the potholes ahead.

EARTH TREMOR

Woken by an initial trembling
I experienced the vibrating of the bed,
creak of the wardrobe door
and rattle of windows
at the second, stronger
tremor as half real,
half recall –

quelled
almost instantly
as stability returned.

Birds clamoured, dogs barked,
a lavatory flushed,
and I lapsed

back into sleep...

barely
unsettled

by the fact

that
(it would appear

unshakably evident)

any assumption
underlying a certainty
must be presumed

to be

fault-

free.

EASTER MORNING
BY DRAGALEVTSI MONASTERY

After the all-night Liturgy

Flickering between trees,
ferns, and fallen trunks,

the torrent shoots back into sight,
silvering
the exposed slab of rock

over which it hurtles
to leap
from an upended boulder

and slalom
to the next chicane

over my bare feet
numb with the chill
of melted snow.

Pulling them to the warmth
of dry stone, I let sunlight
and the shadow of soft
beech leaves towel them.

Below, as the water
plummets again,
bubbles spit –

each an entire universe
for a fraction
of a second.

Champagne
for the breaking of the Fast.

AT THE SHRINE OF ST. JOHN OF RILA

i

Through burnished foliage
Adam and Eve
and their murderer and murdered sons
puppet sacred scripture.

Forehead pressed
against cranberry velvet,
I trust
to whatever
salvation might prescribe.

Where the Communists
disposed of the late king's
body, nobody knows.
In the chapel with plain cross
and photo housing his heart
a woman

fractures a cob of bread
and invites us to eat.

ii

The reservation
is the whole of the mountain.
Enter the forest

and instantly
the music from the car park
becomes inaudible.

But where once
were only beasts and flowers,
information panels identify
plants for every complaint

and warn
against summer footwear:

blessed John's nephew
ran off
to join his uncle here

but was kidnapped
back by the tyrant his father,

whereat the hermit besought heaven
to preserve him
and a snake bit him
(the boy)

and he died.
Or did not,
that's the point.

iii

A tiny gilded
sword parries
every approach.

Though the king
came for counsel,
the man of God would not
leave his rock.

Life coils neatly
in the obvious –
a crust broken
at a prime tourist
location where body
parts

of saint
and sovereign
keep rendezvous

and naïf carving
tempts us

to think natural
a day's outing
to the wilderness.

———

Now a World Heritage Site, Rila monastery stands in a protected nature reserve and is a major tourist attraction as well as a place of continuing devotion and pilgrimage. It was founded by disciples of the tenth-century hermit John of Rila, from whom amongst many others Tsar Peter I reputedly sought advice. John's relics are preserved at the monastery. Also interred in the monastery church is the heart of Tsar Boris III, who died in 1943, probably poisoned. His body, buried separately, was exhumed during the Communist period and taken to a secret location, still unknown.

NEW VALUES

Restoration work on Biserica Adormirii Maicii Domnului

Our neighbour of the Dormition
of the Mother of God
is being restored.
Men scale the pine heavens

at home
with their mystery.

Yet domes of the transcendent
are not maintained for love alone –
a month before the elections

the *Primăriă* has released
long-promised cash
for patrimony (hand-outs
for the local street children's centre
and old people's home too).

Perhaps even
democracy
has its mystical side.

Earthquake and frost survivors,

the domes shine bright
with new zinc scales

like the armour of the Archangel Michael.

—
Primăriă: mayor's office.

CERNICA MONASTERY

Hands like vine leaves
against a blood-dark sun
aim the inevitable device...

but better a memory
stored to ferment
like plum cloud

with the croaking of frogs
over the promontory.

A thrush
in silhouette
on a marble cross

catalyses the process that
with trigger and whirr
we would adulterate.

Mosquitoes feed
as we return

from the tombs of possible
saints, certain martyrs,
and the confessor

whose grave
we had come
to honour.

A mother
of four puppies
growls as we pass.

COME HOME, DADA

Lodged
in timber
two
caryatids

await conservation
in the amuse*um*
of the street.

Otiose pediment,
shingled ogee!
Let me

apostrophise you

before the next bull
departs – your insouciance
(killing
in its day)

be ravished

and a rosette
be pinned to your
ah!
chipped bosom.

PIAȚA VICTORIEI

i

Christmas lights and ploughed
snow confuse the traffic

that wheels about this irregular-shaped
stadium where wind-chill forces
the temperature to historic lows.

Across from the Cold War
Government building
the BRD tower airbrushes
night with dazzle.

Come spring
the brick canopy of *Muzeul Țăranului*
and the spiked finial of the Geological
Museum roof in Kiseleff Park
float on a bubble-bath of green.

On the west side of the square,
enticed by a banner promising
'live reptiles',
children tug grandparents to the G. Antipa
Museum of Natural History.

ii

Memory alone, however,
curates the occasion when,
seeing our taxi meter
clocking double
while stationary at the lights,
Dana (Nam-wounded)
informed the driver
we were bailing out.

I had one foot
on the tarmac already
when the şofer revved
and let in the clutch...

till Dana roared him down
and he hit the brakes.

Over the tyre-thunder,
with foreigner fluency,
we called out his skulduggery.

'See that?' fumed
the veteran. 'Braked
so damn hard the bird's cage
fell on the floor...'

Gently he tsk-tsked
through the bars
to his flustered parrot.
'... then just flung her into the road!'

iii

And my homage alone
immortalises
the government clerks,
the hunger strikers
and *jandarmerie*,
the drivers of the 783, the flower
vendors, the morning commuters
queuing for *plăcintă cu mere*
at the top of Lascăr Catargiu.

iv

Arena of hustle,
dealing, gesture,
skid of the moment,
caesura of record...

where the blast of a police
whistle is drowned

by the mimetic crooning
of a colourful
survivor.

———

*Muzeul Țăranului: Bucharest's famous Peasant Museum celebrating the
traditional life and customs of rural Romania.*
Plăcintă cu mere: a sweet pastry like an apple turnover.

URBAN ORPHEUS

Dogs pant beneath cars
in the heat of day,
emerging at night
to patrol their territory.

Nice Cerberus!
Please don't bite…
The underworld slavers
with neo-rococo ornament.

Past dolphin-nosed drainpipe
and dripping air-con,
through an archway
into a courtyard

with cracked ceramic
throne and empty washing line,

sight and sound make way
for a must of dead plaster.

And music charms

the door
to the cellar steps.

LIVING IN THE END TIMES

The laminated A4 earthquake
procedure issued by the Embassy,
prominent against the dark
panelling of the church lobby,
always startles locals who
have lived their whole lives
without such advice.

Last Holy Week
I stuck a palm cross behind it.
Some time in the Easter season it was removed –
perhaps someone thought it untidy.
Or frivolous. Of course
I know a twist of dried leaf
will hardly protect us
come 'the big one'.

This year I left the card
(red print, liturgically correct)
unadorned.

Those guilty of stripping the trees
and blaspheming
on Palm Sunday
experienced a quake
(or two? accounts differ)
at the end of the week
and start of the new.

And we trumpet
'Thine be the glory...', tune
Handel. And the rent veil
was replaced long ago.

Barely aged
the notice remains,
familiarity dulling alarm.
The building has withstood many
a shake after all, and those
without Embassy protection
swap anecdotes of survival.

Luck? Providence?

Ritual may be no
substitute for health
and safety

yet still I see the folded top
of that palm cross
poking above the
procedure

and feel
its absence

like a rumble
and roar of stone.

RESPECTS

Gathered about the flagpole
we remember the victims of the bombings.
A few words, two minutes' awkwardness,
and the day's business can resume.

Should anyone wish to gun us down
the enhanced security in their dun
uniforms beyond the railings
could not prevent them. Remember,
O dust and ashes,
that what makes life worth living
sits compact in the chest,
does not pad out one's clothing,
does not cause one to glance
this way and that, clench-jowled.

A floral arrangement
like an ice-cream *bombe* is removed
from the balustrade, and neither hate
nor stoicism, fear nor a job to be done,
can efface the emptiness of the stone
or the mown grass growing.

SOFIA: REMEMBERING

*Each November the British, French, German, and Italian
Embassies in Sofia organised a joint Remembrance commemoration at
the main city cemetery, where alongside the Bulgarian civilian graves,
military graves are arranged in separate plots according to nationality.
A military padre was flown in to conduct the British part of the ceremony.*

Rain easing...

(I knew only of the November
Armistice, yet here headstones read
December, some even 1919.)

'My mother's maiden
name was rather unusual...'

We hurry on
to the adjacent German plot.

'... and I noticed a stone with
her name on. Right regiment.
We know three of the family died.'

But I am distracted
from attending to the lady
with whom I share an umbrella:
the bugler had gone straight
into 'Reveille' then observed
barely a minute's silence
before sounding 'The Last Post'.

Too much to bear, the screams

through the downpour?

Speeches, wreaths,
and *Vater unser*
are offered amid black memorials
as the rain threatens a comeback –

umbrellas mushroom again,
bargain telescope nudging
dress Stewart, Balmain
autograph jabbing *Evrofutbol.*

Then briskly on once more
to the French military acre,
past broken masonry,
unkempt trees, and ivy in Bulgarian
civvy street. I note a soldier
in cherry trousers and plumed
képi dashing ahead of us
the other side of the wall.

Discreet conversations about
re-drawn boundaries
accompany our arrival at a place
where stars and crescents
punctuate the ranked crosses.

We donate for *bleuets*
to pin beside our poppies,
as an elderly Assumptionist
from Plovdiv does the honours.

It is only by the grace of God
the heavens have not opened upon us.
Then wreaths at the Italian memorial.

There has, it appears, been friction
between the Italians and French –
the Italian number two is here,
but traditionally they have held
their own ceremony. Next year
all will be done together
to better represent
the European idea.

Over *Glühwein* at the German
Embassy afterwards
I discuss French *laïcité*
and English county regiments.

But at a suitable moment
I must point out to the DA
that Resurrection is not
a prelude to mourning –
'The Last Post' should sound
before (as it is properly called)
'Rouse'.

And that second minute
should never be skimped.

Meanwhile I need
myself to remember
the history I learned at school

skimped
on others' truths.

TRADE: A STUDY ON THE ECONOMY OF THE INCARNATION

i

Prisoners held in the Black Mosque
after the Liberation
sold beadwork where stalls

strung along the pavement
from what is now the church
of Sveti Sedmochislenitsi

are piled with dates, almonds,
raspberries, agate yellow raisins...

I bargain with history –
lantern-jawed and crook-limbed –
at the corner of Tsar Shishman
for a hand-woven blanket.

Outside St. Nicholas the Miracle-Maker
a Brezhnev comedy act
opens his mac and growls,
'Cigars? Beluga caviar?'

These three endure:
bootleg,
excess production,
the real McCoy.

ii

No empire from the East
diverts a river
to cut us off

as we intone, 'Strengthen
for service, Lord, the hands
that holy things have taken'

from books fussing
in pernickety italics,
Perhaps by
Ephraim the Syrian.

And bread and merlot
in the Residence basement
is hardly the catacombs –

contract security
guards monitor
the compound.

Ephraem Syriacus,
haste to our aid!

iii

Byzantine, Ottoman,
Romanov, British,
Soviet...

Where the body is,
there the eagles will gather.
A deliberately obscure
saying? Luke 17.37.

My hymnbook exchange

(Bucharest's 'Old and New'
gifted by a Lancashire parish
years ago now transferred to Sofia,
Bucharest having recently received
St. Mary Twickenham's
'Ancient & Modern New Standard
Revised' upon that church's
purchase of new hymnals)

hardly compares in weight
with arms deals
and infrastructure contracts.
Yet Ephrem's 'flowery'
verses mightily fortified
besieged Nisibis.

iv

Surveillance
is the new
empire.

v

An English-language
guide sheet commends
the former Black Mosque's
architectural 'constriction'.

Our anamnesis
is of the most
extreme constriction.

At street stalls
timeless scales
are brandished
for chilli and pumpkin alike

yet experts
can no longer
tell original
from fake.

Lean days around the corner.

'Feet that tread
thy holy courts...' we sing,
'... from light
do thou not banish...'

vi

At the Ali Baba's cave
of the museum shop
I buy (to make my visit
real) a reproduction
of a ceramic goblet
from the First Bulgarian Empire,

a garish postcard
of a man in horned mask
and goat skins at the festival
of St. Trifon Zarezan
and the god Dionysus,

and two bars
of rose petal soap.

In south-east Europe, the concept of empire is linguistically more embedded than that of kingdom. The 'kingdom' of heaven – Greek 'basileia' – is in Bulgarian 'tsarstvo', in Romanian 'împărăţie' – 'empire' – of heaven. Where appearance, negotiation, and pragmatism hold sway, how is authenticity established? The economy (in the theological sense) of the Incarnation is lived out through the exchanges of a social and personal economy of gifts and goods in which, beyond the poles of disabling power and disabling subservience, transcendent love is the only touchstone of value. St. Ephrem the Syrian's hymns (mid-fourth century) were sung as the forces of imperial Persia besieged his native city of Nisibis. His poetry tends to be dismissed as 'florid' by Westerners, still shaped by the affluence and security of imperial and post-imperial societies. Yet it had a power that derived from something more than marketable and traded invention – something other than ever more closely measured and regulated observation.

METAMORPHOSIS

A donkey cart
lurching under its load
of mud and straw bricks

presents a picture postcard
hazard on the coastal
road where maxi-taxis
ply between Black Sea resorts.

Numbness easing from
emergency dentistry
in Mangalia, I wonder
at marble columns, Tanagra
statuettes, and opalescent flasks
in the museum of ancient Callatis,
explore stumps of fortification
rooted in the jaw of the coast,

and lard myself with mud
hawked by Roma women
as jealous of their pitches
as gulls over a dropped
dobrogeană. The therapy requires

you stand cruciform,
gazing at the dolphinless sea,
letting the loam bake
before (forget Tanagra –
a crude votive at most)

dashing into the waves
to know the transformation
from buffoon to god!

Then with bitter tears
for no-show dolphins

it's a maxi-taxi
back to our village,
where the green and pink
fisherman's cottages
are being extracted

and replaced
with multi-storey implants.

Lamenting the loss
of the picturesque,
yet free of pain,
all numbness gone,

I urge fortitude.
'No more weeping now!'
Embrace exile,
buy the postcard.

Mangalia: south of Constanţa (ancient Tomis), where the Roman poet Ovid was exiled. The dark local mud is reputedly rich in medicinal qualities.
Dobrogeană: a cheese and egg pastry local to the Dobrogea region.

ROCKET SCIENCE

An exercise in devaluation

Newspapers are full
of the imminent transition
to the *Leu greu* (four noughts
to be knocked off the currency).

Paying our apartment
service charge I muddle
my millions and hundreds of thousands.

Then... change from the cleaner's
till receipts, 478,000. Bread rolls
at the baker's, 31,000 (lose two
of those flibbertigibbet 500 coins,
always a pleasure). But
it is the old lady with her snowdrops
at the street corner who
brings me to grief.

Darned headscarf, feet
in clouts, she accosts
without aggression – 10,000
for two. Bunches. Amid the white drops
a rogue star, bright blue.

Sensing my arithmetical paralysis,
she is about to reduce the price.
I try to deflect her. 'Ten bunches!'
(floundering with ten times

two for 10,000). Then we both
speak together: 'How much is that?'
'That's from me...' She adds
another bunch. The problem ratchets.

'You really... don't know?'
I detect a mild note almost of fear
in her voice. But the panic
is mine. How many gaps in those
teeth? 100,000 cannot be excessive.

Her prayer for God to grant me
health is a shriving, my penance
being to re-learn
the value
of what is quantifiable.

Leu greu: the Leu ('lion') is the Romanian currency; 'greu' means 'heavy'.

DISCERNING THE JOY

Thick cloud over the Carpathians
had depressed our excitement about the jaunt.
But once through the Prahova valley,
and having bettered the self-contradictory
signage around Braşov, the mountains
became visible in the distance
on our left as we headed west,
and our spirits rose.

Stilt-legged in nests
on concrete pylons,
storks belied the fragility
of domestic bliss.

Women in voluminous skirts
leaned with balletic
balance into the road,
flagging small white tubs at us –
wild raspberries to gorge
on by the fistful as we drove.

Turning south off the main road,
we were a curiosity
for dames yarning on benches
by yard gates. Children in short
jackets and broad-brimmed hats
stopped their football to wave.

At the next village we slowed
to the amble of cows and buffalo
returning from pasture.

Regaining speed around
a bend, we had to brake sharply
for another slow-lumbering herd
driven by a boy with an ornate
bullwhip over one shoulder –
which at sight of us he cracked
over the beasts' rumps,
goading them to a scamper.
As they ran they butted and
mounted each other. The boy
skipped behind, upping
the misbehaviour with further crackerjack
whipshots, grinning back at us
for approbation.

The beasts cantered ahead
raising a storm of dust,
the boy sprinting after them
with whoops and shouts.
At the crest of a rise, where washing
hung between neglected blockhouses,
men, women, and children ran out
hollering and waving their arms
to corral the delinquents
now scattering in all directions
among the ruins of systematisation.

Hardly a prayerful prelude
to our arrival at Sâmbătă monastery
where we had arranged to spend the night,
and which we reached through acres
of collectivised orchard – unpruned trees,
gaunt as gallows, mocking the few
brought back into production by the monks.

*

Swallows zipped between
the brothers' living quarters
and the sculpted eaves of the church
at the centre of the enclosure.
The *stareț* welcomed us and was
at once interrupted by his mobile phone.
From behind the church came a young
monk drumming on a plank nestled
yoke-like into his shoulder.
As the hammering quickened
a couple of scarfed women
emerged from the gatehouse.
Three brothers joined them.

Difficult to say from where,
a crowd had congregated.
The church was packed.

In the *pridvor* with its
frescoes of the Crisis
(wheels of fire, wing-motored,
at the foot of a throne; to the right
the river of flame and ladder
of ascent, Belial like a deformed carp
at the bottom consuming the *commedia*,
snouted demons and adolescent minotaurs
prodding the damned with *commedic* glee,
and to the left the aesthetic disaster
of paradise, with its male/female
imbalance and stockade
and a single tree fruiting
in miraculous strangeness)

people shifted foot occasionally
as lamplight, incense, and chant
flowed into the dusk
and the mountains
became silhouette.

At the end of the office,
on the arm of a brother,
the blind *duhovnic* Teofil,
Lover-of-God,
shuffled out from the light.

*

All night the frogs
by the conference-centre-cum-guesthouse
had chorused. I struggled
into a pious frame of mind
for the Liturgy.

Barbs of black-blue flame
flashed through the mist.
The morning congregation,
larger than at Vespers, overflowed
from the church, loudspeakers
transmitting the service.
The Preparation was already over.

As sunlight leavened the day
Teofil evoked his mother
kneading dough… Woe to you,
Scribes! Reject the stock
polarity of saint and pharisee,
still one is left with hunger.
'And who, when asked,
would deny their child bread?'

At the healing fountain a family
filled 8-litre containers with water,
while behind, unremarkable
as a boulder, a monk
knelt under a tree.

We said our farewells
and the magic began.

*

Sun sweeping remnants of haze
from the mountains, buffalo
wallowing shoulder-high in mud,
raptors suspended
like demagnetised compass-needles,
we picked cross-country

to the main road and off again
toward the wall of trees,
rising turf, and rock that led to the pass.
The Transfăgărăşan
is open only about six weeks of the year.
To cross it, we had been told,
you need good brakes.

The bends were assembled
like old-fashioned scalextric.
Behind and below us the plateau expanded,
while against the grandeur of stone and sky
crumbling concrete culverts inspired
diminishing confidence.

Where the tarmac entered a tunnel
for the final passage into Wallachia,
tables in slush-spattered snow
touted sheepskins and knitwear,
weavings midway between craft and tat,
Kodak film, and cheese in pine bark canisters.

Water and snow, like distant cousins,
observed their differences
in the navel of Bâlea Lac.
We sallied down to the lake's edge
and contemplated its temperature,
depth, and blackness, thinking
vacant curiosity no violation.

As we sat in the sun
outside the wooden *cabană*
for beer and *mici*, a priest we had seen
at the monastery came and spoke to us,
snooker-black hair tied in a ponytail,

purple glass cufflinks catching
on tailored sleeves. His card
gave two New York addresses...

Time to press on.

*

The next three hours
were spent hunting for the car keys.

The power of the place
(or Cufflinks?)
had vaporised them.

When you have mislaid your car keys
on top of a mountain
no possibility is entirely unbelievable.

A thick fret enveloped us.
We prayed for the coded
answer to life's single problem
to reveal itself at our feet.

'What,' mused Simon
as we converged in the opaque limbo,
'might Teofil say in our situation?
I think he might ask, "Where is the joy?"'
'I don't see much joy in the situation,'
snapped Angela.

Retreating to the *cabană*
for council and coffee laced with *coniac*,
we resolved after dismissing

a series of joyless
alternatives to summon a taxi
from Sibiu to return us to Bucharest –

I to catch a plane for Sofia
first thing next morning,
Angela to face Wim
and pick up the spare key,
and Simon to welcome as a discipline
at the end of his retreat

this jape
of the imp of the Făgăraş.

---

*Systematisation/Collectivisation: Ceauşescu's devastating continuation
of the Stalinist project to replace individual smallholder farming with a
system of massive state-owned co-operatives.*

*Sâmbătă monastery in the foothills of the Făgăraş mountains was
founded in the late seventeenth century and played an important part
in preserving Orthodoxy in Transylvania, where papal authority was
asserted in the eighteenth century. Ruined and restored over many years,
it even continued to undergo restoration work during the Communist
period.*

Stareţ: the abbot of a monastery.

*Pridvor: the colonnaded verandah-porch to a traditional Romanian
Orthodox church, usually richly frescoed.*

Duhovnic: a spiritual guide.

*Transfăgărăşan: a spectacular, but essentially functionless, road built
over the Făgăraş mountains, in the southern Carpathians, during the
Communist period.*

Mici: traditional meatballs grilled over charcoal.

CONTRARY FORCES

Trees tug in an indecisive wind.

Sparse lights
indicate a village

otherwise
only a honey-gleaming
moon two days from
full keeps lawlessness
at bay.

Clouds pincer –
from the left a flank
of basalt advancing
on a wind-torn mane
streaming from the right.

The gap between
contracts.

Lightning clamps.

The still just asymmetric
disk is wiped

from the sky.
Sporadic
violet flashes

traverse
total night.

FENCE OF AN ABANDONED VILLA

Green metal palings
devoured
by the tree
they once railed –

vegetable

lips
smack.

A MATURE LIME BEING STRANGLED BY A WISTERIA

Languorous,
stealthy,
the wisteria
sprawls up into the tree,

mauve tongues
licking the pale bark
and barely leafing branches,

till in a burst
of vigour it claims
total possession –

pendulous blooms

a killer
pelt of purple.

IMPROVISATION

Four strings
of morning glory

rise from a square metre
of weeds, dried dog turds,
and bent metal

for day to improvise upon,
to pluck notes
of un-self-flaunting blue
and green-sheathed
progressions

nosing out tomorrow
as yesterday
arrives already by noon.

The cadence
of each day's movement:
beauty, ever memorable,
never repeatable.

From a theme
all crude necessity,
dull vigour,
natural erosion

this interpenetration of soil
and light
along four cords
stretched by an anonymous
instrument-maker

lodges eternity
in our matter.

FOR WANT OF A CARPET TACK

In honour of a gentleman observed in Sofia standing in the middle of intersecting tramlines picking his teeth

James Ramsay

O polly wolly doodle
all the day!

Hair frizzed
either side
of the vanity mirror
in which he picks his teeth

the Banjo
jangles
a railed world.

Till a bell-clappering
tram bears down, and…

hoppity twang,
my fairy fey!

(*Gadje!* Disapprobation
snaps like the click
of a powder compact.)

Fare thee well!

In a vault
over charged wires

he's off
for to see his Suzyanna.

HEATHROW 8/7/05

James Ramsay

Like a trail of black blood
the lead from the young
executive's earplugs
trickles to the player
which pumps his body
forward and back
as he consumes
his paper (gripped taut
between white-knuckle fists)
at the departure gate.
Pinstripes momentarily
recover authority
as he sits bolt upright,
addressing his fellow passengers
with a blank stare.
Then (next track?)
he jerks forward again
into the coarse-pixelled mayhem
at Liverpool Street and Tavistock Square,
head-banging a conditioned space
in which... rage? grief? impotence?
what does he carry?
are limited
to a single permitted item.

SUNDAY CONSTITUTIONAL

Medusa hair and God-fearer
beard, rucksack festooned
with empty water bidons...
his pink plastic mac
flutters unbuttoned

in the wind
by the top of the ski
lift where snow fell last week
and has now largely melted.

At the foot of Vitosha,
the trees just starting to turn,
girls waited
alone on the ring road.

Here above the treeline,
with a view of Sofia
off-white in the sun,
clouds skim
the boulder-strewn summit.

The gale blasts city piety.

We return to the protective trees
where others also take
their Sunday constitutional,
and the prophet is feeding a cur.

Then as we drive back down
from the start of the ski lift
and the thermometer rises,
leaves revert from rust and copper
to green and saffron.
Sacred violence
becomes a concept.

No girls now.

Above a half-constructed
villa the national flag

hangs limp
in a windless dusk.

THE BASKET-MAKER

Down Fall of the Bastille Street,
a raw wind whipping dust
into the whitening cherry trees,

a creature of cane –

swaying pillar
of plaited trays,
waisted panniers,
hooped chargers, tubs
to be placed upside
down and danced on –

heads for market
to slough
his winter skin.

A SHAKE-UP
IN THE JUSTICE DEPARTMENT

Official: fat policemen
cannot run after thieves
or catch terrorists. The EU
demands slimline officers

as the government
resigns then withdraws
its resignation over proposed
justice reforms that could land half
the Constitutional Court behind bars.

Armed with phonecard
and carton of Marlboro
I take my turn in the queue
of visitors hoiking provisions
into Rahova penitentiary.

Tattoos pallid on slack
skin, the no-longer-youthful
Brit whose transfer has been
unaccountably held up

waves across the visiting hall.

He tells me a blind
eye is turned
when food is cooked
on wired-up bed springs.

I note the warders
are relatively
lean.

FUNERAL PROCESSION

James Ramsay

A boy in a black suit
struggling with a four-foot-high cross
slung with wreath and name sash

leads a solemn pavane
of men, all similarly black-suited,
taking up half the street.

A priest
in requisite glad rags
walks ahead of a Luton van –
driver hunched, balancing
the clutch – followed
by black-shawled women
nursing beads and gladioli.

The van is open at the rear.

Through the bus window
I have a privileged view
of the unlidded coffin:
aquiline nose pointing

above the number plate
to a fibreglass sky.

In front of me
schoolgirls cross themselves
and resume their jokes.

MONUMENTS
TO A STOLEN REVOLUTION

Bucharest 2004

I

89s
cut in white marble

tumble
like locks
by the airport access road –

this fifteenth anniversary
memorial a lesson
in the learning process of revolution.

i

Far cry
from the roughly
carpentered timber

that until recently
stood in Piaţa Romană,
near where Romulus and Remus
in replica suckle fratricide

and where the dead are now honoured
in seasoned oak,
crafted with the grain
of exhaustible matter.

Dream and riddle,
disturbance, deceit,

monumental on a personal scale,
breathing mountain air
through fossil-driven urgency.

ii

Outside the National Theatre,
like a troupe of actors,
ten stone crosses
march north
from Kilometer Zero,

traffic pumping,
lapsing, spurting
through their veins

while across from the Intercontinental
(new creation, grace of capital)
a bleached fascia announces:
Association of the Victims
of the *Mineriade*... those
murderous covert twitches of authority.

What constitutes a hero?
Wreaths laid on whitewash.

iii

Meanwhile in Revolution
Square the Martyr of Sighet
turns cracked torso
to THE balcony

from which, a dozen years
on, Dubya guaranteed God's
favour upon Romania
as he invaded Iraq.

Below the balcony
marigolds
in a stone triangle –
fury of a wasp
under the skin of an apple.

At the centre of this square
a workmanlike calvary

for all victims of communism,
'48 to '89,
in washed-out red, yellow,
and blue, a large 'O' unpainted
(excision of the imperialist logo),
oracle of the rising and cutting off of the sap.
Sometimes flowers are offered
or votives lit in the flimsy tabernacle.
Once I noticed an unwrapped bar
of chocolate whitening.

And opposite the former
royal palace (with now pristine façade
as befits the monstrance

of the national art treasures)
Humanitas bookshop

retains its vermiculation of shell
damage – wounds enquiry can burrow
into, never deep enough.

While still unremediated,
the rear walls of the palace
tell the same tale.
What price hope?

Sport and loans
pacify the constituency.

II

Black cavalcades with flashing
lights and outriders
no longer bring traffic to a halt.
Yet those who fight corruption

can be subverted
by the vision that is their purity of heart.

i

Hair continues to grow
after death.
A body neatly laid out

when living
was perhaps never so groomed.

A thirty-something computer
programmer, close-cropped,
hankers for Canada, Australia,
normality, a world

of opportunities
and fewer memorials.

ii

Behind a closed up
bus ticket kiosk
outside the Faculty of Architecture,
on dawn-pink marble
memorialising those who 'died
for freedom in December '89',
gelled after the word *libertate*...
a black question mark

like a hair out of place.

iii

And always a jolt,
on B-dul Balcescu...
that stump cross of iron
piping, trefoils welded
at the top and end of each arm,
anchored in the pavement
between the Tropical Club

and Eden Hairdressing,
with above it on the wall
photos set in marble, black
and white shocks,
beneath bleached colours
and the angry void
still unfilled.

So I read to the left
of the 19-year-old
who was first to be taken out
in Bucharest that Advent,
and of the other twelve who,
'kneeling in prayer for
the souls of those killed in Timişoara',
went with him. Salon Eden's
A-board has been stuck
smack in front of funerary
periods stiff with restraint
to the right. I cannot read what they say.

In need of a haircut, I ascend
to Paradise on the 2nd floor
via an alcove half taken up
by a book stall – and emerge,
years younger, to see
the A-board has been shifted,
leaving the inscription more visible.
(Engrossed in a book,
the man at the bookstall
does not look up.)

'More than ten years on,' I scan easily
now, 'our eyes have no more tears.
There can be no peace until those

guilty of taking what was not theirs
are brought to account.'

III

A monument that was to have been unveiled
in the final hours of office of the president
'who had a major role in the Revolution'
has been refused planning permission
by the mayor.

How resist
cynicism
or empty statement?

A line must be drawn
under historical events,
as a razor scrapes
the back of the neck.

i

Fashions swing
against walls
patinaed with graffiti.
Careers are confirmed
in the art of revolution.

'*Iisus* is coming! Repent!'
has been added in magenta
below the question mark.

A certain expenditure
is now required.
While those who resigned
when the miners were bussed in,
or who declined their sop of hero's soil,
have never permitted themselves to mourn
nor let their beard grow
for the stipulated time.

The revolution was permitted,
so I have heard,
by those fed up
with having nothing
to spend their money on.

An unbound generation,
eyes gouged,
looks to heaven
and hears the scoffing.

ii

But twisted remains

will light truth
in the flesh
of those who come after.

Mineriade: a series of anti-government demonstrations that took place after the interim government (largely made up of Communist party politicians) tasked with organising democratic elections following the 'kangaroo court' trial and execution of the Ceauşescus formed itself into a political party, claiming to represent democracy. Agents provocateurs from the Communist Securitate were involved in inciting violence, and thousands of miners from western Romania were brought into Bucharest to 'defend democracy'. The clashes resulted in many injuries and fatalities.

Martyr of Sighet: Iuliu Maniu, a key political figure in inter-war Romania, sought to establish a patriotic yet also pluralist democracy in the face of both Fascism and Soviet Communism. He died in 1953 in the infamous Sighet prison, and was buried in the common grave there. Among numerous martyrs of Sighet, he offers a secular, ecumenical witness with which – as the fame of this 'broken man' statue testifies – many sympathise.

WALLPAPER TV

I note with embarrassment
the mud on my shoes, having
walked from the end of the line
to this ex-dissidents' reunion
in the Street of Quietness.

Orthodox Easter being
five weeks after ours this year,
the priest from Colțea church
in University Square
is still fasting.

'But if you say it is Easter...'
He raises a glass.

Our Roman hosts assure him
the victory has been won.

On the screen in the corner of the room
Animal World
regales us with the mating
difficulties of the Arctic viper.

Painted eggs are cracked.
The Orthodox shell remains intact.
'Proof,' I adduce, 'of the triumph
of Orthodoxy.'

The Orthodox priest's mute
driver gives a thumbs-up.

'Those who didn't experience
Communism can have no idea
what it was like.'

The fearsome
leverage of certain animals' jaws
is now the subject of the superb
photography, which accompanies
sarmale and village wine.

A package of food
is taken to someone at the door.

I gesture to a photo
honoured with a small glass of daffodils
standing on the TV.
'Who's that?'

A man who until now has been silent
reaches for the plastic frame.
'Padre Pio.' He sets the icon
down by the potatoes. 'He has recently
been beatified. Though no-one
takes much notice. Saints are
after all just like any of us.'

'But more so,'
another voice suggests.

Having watched a female praying
mantis devour her mate
during copulation,
the presenter is now investigating
how far animals can communicate

telepathically with humans
and even read our minds.

Colțea had been closed down
three years before '89,
but when the Revolution started
the priest went in,
rang the bells,
and sang the full Christmas Liturgy.

'And now we have capitalism.'
All turn to me.

Another bottle of wine.

This is our experience.
The mud will wash easily enough
from the tiles.

But how protect ourselves
from that lioness

repeatedly lunging
in slow motion
at the hindquarters of a wildebeest?

---

*Sarmale: traditional festive dish of rice or minced meat wrapped in vine
or cabbage leaves.*

FOR THE DIGNITY
OF THE WHOLE BODY

The sight of workmen rinsing hands and forearms
at the hose by the construction site
took me back to last winter, when night
and day a pipe two feet in diameter
disgorged water into the gutter...
Digging an underground
carpark, they had tapped a spring
that had to be pumped up and into
the sewer. The rushing
siphoned a bucolic strangeness
into the heart of the city.
With night temperatures seventeen
below, the flow steamed
like a spa. Once chemical
analysis had guaranteed it safe,
from the surrounding flats people sallied
with pans and bowls to scrub, brush teeth...
'I mean, in the middle
of a capital city?'
Take a man's pride.
Let pile driving, shifting of earth,
pouring of concrete commence
before dawn where that *fin-de-siècle*
villa with vine-mantled courtyard
was flattened in a matter of minutes.
'OK, period architecture,
but who honestly wants
a heap of bricks
that might fall down
at the next earthquake?'

A new concept occupies
the site, divorced from swag and *coquetterie*.
With temperatures now touching 40,
dust peppers the trickle of water
slinking, as if in shame, along the gutter.
'What this country needs
is a strong middle class.'

THE LAST JUDGEMENT

Matthew 26.44-45

Fleshed in parings,
maggots
and bones,

in coat of moth
sutured with string,

from a dumpster
across the road

up pops
eternity.

SLEEPING DRUNK

Recalling the Pietà d'Avignon

An accordioned body
lapped in concrete,
shards of fallen stucco,
and bent iron

lies inert amid
the roots of an acacia.

That rig of limbs,
extension of arm,
collapse of legs,
is disturbingly familiar.

I first saw it
unsignposted
in the Louvre
at a careless age.

It struck against
the flint certainties
of my mind.

Easier to not see
here the elegance –

default tolerance alone
for spices,
no flowered alabaster.

Gilt spars shaft
through thin branches

onto eyes
not entirely sealed
in stupor or death.

THE BEAUTY OF THE FEMALE FORM

Erected over the phone kiosk
under whose dome in foul
weather the bag lady stands,
an ad for fancy lingerie.

They appeared around the same time,
the black silk-sheathed
three-quarter leg

and the newly homeless
woman seated rod-backed
on the *belle époque* steps nearby

where she slept and shrieked.

After some weeks,
purged of anger,
yogic, she squats
under a tree by the *metrou*.

When rain drives,
the booth offers no refuge
for slippered feet.

But as we pass with flowers –
Dragă! compensation
for a beastly day! –

surely we may appreciate
the beauty
of the female form?

———

Dragă: darling.

RELIC OF A SAINT IN THE NATIONAL HISTORY MUSEUM, SOFIA

Cased in silver filigree
set with beryls

intruder alarmed

this piece of human detritus
has sat behind glass
since the Sixties.

Starting loud
as the river,
the song of the crickets
grows deafening.

We remain mute,
each with our
catalogue entry.

Relocation
has been discussed
for years.

THE WORD

Ears still resounding
with the crashing of the Inhospitable Sea
and the sound of larks and cicadas
on the Kaliakra peninsula

we down home-distilled rakia
and – *Nazdrave!* – talk –
Noroc! – of holy inebriation.

The holiest incapacity
I remember
was one Sunday
in St. Nectan's, Welcombe,
North Devon. No more than half
a dozen of us in church. A retired
priest, former physics teacher,
spoke of crystals
growing along a thread
suspended in solution.

A peacock butterfly beat
against the diamond window
lights as old Scraggy-Neck
addressed us from his box

like a bird thrilling
above the hawk-menaced
reserve of Kavarna

for no better reason than
that he had a voice: and
because fire will devour
this planet, the universe
scroll shut in however
many billion years,
if not this afternoon,
and because the EU
will prohibit *rahat*

and because Allah
gave milk, wine, honey,
and surely music
and love
for us to enjoy

and the capacity to delight
in a swell shattering
to crystal
against rocks suspended
in time,
each with its structure
marvellously made.

ULTIMATE MEANING

En route to the children's hospice
my phone rings. 'May you live,
Father!' *Părintele* Gheorghe sounds
agitated. 'With most particular respect,
where are you?' 'But it doesn't begin
till half-past.' 'We want to start early...'

I am stuck in a taxi.
The traffic inches forward.
'*Imediat.*'

A sticker
on the rear of the taxi in front
reads, 'Is there life after death?
Climb in and find out.'
I and the taxi driver debate

this message as we swerve
through side-streets
and around potholes
and dislodged cobbles,
and pull up with a screech of brakes
only ten minutes late. The VIPs
have yet to arrive.

*

Two nurses carry children
in their arms. Unbleached
candles and incense are lit.
Pr. Gheorghe wriggles

into his blue and silver
vestments while the cantor,
his son, arranges markers in a book.

At some point, I know,
I shall be invited to say
'a few words'. But who
can speak for these children

with their long limbs
and eyes focussed on the ceiling?
I do not assume
they cannot understand.

We are doused with water
from an aspergillum of basil.

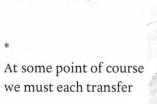

*

At some point of course
we must each transfer

to another mode of transport –

and find out
that fragrance, azure and argent,
flung water drops,

voice and gesture

are themselves
entirely

the subject
of their own meaning.

A PROBLEM WITH AUTHORITY

Texting, elbows on knees,
school satchel
like a deformation on his back,

the teenager is approached
by a guard
barely older than he.

'Take off your bag
when you sit
in the *metrou*.'

The command is repeated.

Shuffling his satchel
onto the empty seat beside him
without looking up

the offender
continues texting.

For a while
the guard lingers.

Then thrusting thumbs
under belt
off he

sways

down the tract
of interconnected
carriages.

EPIPHANY

Brandishing tinfoil stars
on sticks with glued-on
Nativity icon cards,
children beg
without sparkle.

Is it wise to give?
The Magi unwittingly
precipitated a massacre.

Innocence is pure at a distance.
Seeing the constellation
so near is unnerving.

The closeness
with which their eyes
elicit response
prompts... disgust?
Anger? Kindness will not placate
the manager in the wings.
Compassion should guide,
not goad.

I dither.

ENTER from the East
down the escalator
a Magus –

shiny night-blue cloak
riding behind him,
hair a manger of hay,
waving a snooker cue
tipped with outsize tinfoil star.
Like a firework he tears
along the platform

then back against the surge of people
as the train draws to a stop. In
he leaps, two carriages down.

Already the children
are working their new clientèle.

Two schoolgirls have a fit of the giggles
as we gather speed through
a starless tunnel.

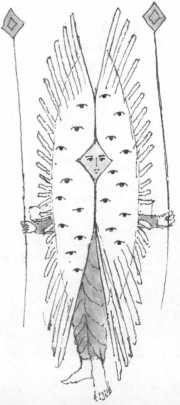

KEEP MUSIC LIVE

'Knock, knock, knockin'
on heaven's door' echoes
up the escalator
and round the pillars of
Piața Romană *metrou* station.

Technology drives
the unsupported voice
underground.

I recall mortuary
marble shimmering
to kids stupid with glue

tripping each other up
as the eldest bawled
half-remembered songs...

A *paznic* silences
the busker.

Working real time –
a dimension
at risk of extinction –
not that far from
heaven, a little below
street level,
he starts the refrain once more.

A trundle and push
of warm air
signal the approach
of the next train.

And in the two seconds
before the doors open
and we step aboard

we hear only
the song
defying

the undead.

SEEING AND NOT SEEING

Each morning I check
the thermometer outside
our bedroom window

but only later
as I descend to the *metrou*
and my glasses mist
in the uplift of warm air

do the runged numbers
start to make sense.

On a mild day like today,
which threatens the residual
heaps of bulldozed snow
in the middle of the square,
I am through the metal doors
at the bottom of the outer steps
and heading already for the first
flight of internal steps

before a haze begins to form
at the perimeter of each
lens – and if a train draws in
as I reach the ticket barrier
I still have vision enough
to take the final steps in twos
and jump into the end carriage.

But on a real
winter day...

vision starts to go
at the top of the external steps.
And pulling open the heavy metal door
I am at once

in the kingdom of the blind –
where I must grope for the wall
and edge forward as I remove
a glove to hunt for my pass
(and if anyone at this juncture
wishes to relieve me of my wallet, *poftiţi*).

Amorphous shapes shamble
and shove about me.
My tactic in the evolutionary
game now is to neither
fumble too awkwardly
nor feign indifference
to my disability,

and crucially
should a train arrive
as I retrieve my pass
from the automatic barrier...

take the final steps

one

at

a

time.

From a bench on an empty platform
I can then at leisure admire
the small bullet
holes of clear glass

that appear at the centre
of each lens and gradually
(depending on the degrees minus)
expand

till equilibrium with
the ambient temperature is reached.
At which point I see at last

what the thermometer
had been telling me.

Poftiți: a courtesy word with various meanings. In this instance perhaps,
'Be my guest!'

NETTLE SALAD DAYS

Sap-quickening
fa-la-la

and re-emergent flesh...

yet for all the blossom-wooing
warmth still
that undertow of the *demi-saison*,
the invisible duenna of harsh times

nudging
a ski-slope-
gilded *jeunesse*.

Clouds blush cherry.
Birdsong drowns the traffic.

A pensioner
at the crossroads
sells handfuls of young
nettles tied with string.

In springtime
half a century ago
traditional techniques
were all they had.
We know better now
(though those who come after
will know better too).

Hormones have ever
outwitted skin and bones.
Let the sentimental feel pity.

These are the years of adventure.
Our age's imperative
to lose one's innocence
to find it.

Or financialise
the fa-la-la —

all mating-call
and turf warning.

PARIS OF THE EAST

Crystal stakes
at every gutter and ledge...

frozen music

to be guillotined off
by the baton stroke
of enlightenment –

when sculpted lintels
shed their myth-shaggy
lashes and stiletto beards

and we may indulge
in a façade

of liberty, equality, and fraternity
free of nightmare.

Early twentieth-century Bucharest was known as 'Little Paris', 'the Paris of the East', much of its architecture showing Parisian influences.
Vlad Țepeș, fifteenth-century ruler of Wallachia, became a byword for cruelty under the nickname of Vlad the Impaler. The guillotine became a symbol of the Terror in Paris.
The image of architecture as 'frozen music' is attributed to either the German philosopher Schelling or Goethe (in conversation with Schiller).

THE SUMMONS

This November of languid
creeper, untrained vine
cascading from a phone line,

carnelian leaf
not clawed
by frost,

grapes at their
most luscious,

hats, scarves,
gloves forgotten:

till yesterday's
sudden deluge
and slap of wind

that set the trees in a panic

as a door
banged to...

Persephone hurrying back
late
to the underworld.

URBAN *PRIMĂVARĂ*

James Ramsay

Forsythia stabs downward
from a window box.

We are ignorant of the earth
under our feet.

In a rictus of hope
asphalt exposes
soil teeming with tiny
filaments and cylinders of green.

A stranger sun injects
pinks, blues, yellows

into me
with drug-free precision

and I am unburdened

of a certainty
I never knew I had.

COMMUTING BUCHAREST-SOFIA

This will become routine,
I thought –

mountain crests
in a Pacific of blue.

Yet for all my trips
I did not see it again:

heartstop
of high pastures
and valleys,

cumulus breaking
on jade green reefs,
yes –

but never
quite

that beauty
from which I shied

at my first descent.

THE THRILL OF FLIGHT

A lectern eagle
of cloud

vomits fire
the far side of heaven.

Roofs
of isolated villages
glint

like marcasite.

Scrumpled
clingfilm, porn-
pink...

The passenger in front
reclines,
I grab my glass
of Sec de Murfatlar.

A hairy forearm
invades my space.

Enough!

Abjure
all phoney gods!

WAITING IN THE INTER-CITY,
EARLY MORNING

Music leaks
like gas
from hidden speakers.

Ice jags
the underbelly of the *personal*
across the platform.

The other side of tinted glass,
disconnected from the world
of fixed armrests,
tabletop beech veneer,
and velcroed-back curtains,

the man tapping the wheels
with long-handled hammer
might be a movie
extra.

I tug the curtain
to no purpose
against the hiss of romance,

nostalgia,
pain,
bliss,

and more romance –

inadequate insulation
against the freezing dawn.

AT THE STREET CHILDREN'S CENTRE

They came back
tired from fishing, excited
by their finds – a fawn

barely a week old
and two tortoises.

Of course the deer
had to be reported
to the *pădurar*
but for a moment

they had a life
to care for,
could rejoice

in improvising
pen and shelter, observing
a tongue no larger
than a cat's

lapping milk...

Whereas those curiosities
that nibbled
their proffered leaves

but were otherwise
as exhausting to mind
as a motionless
float

hared off unwatched –

imparting
through tears
the wisdom of *Esop*.

James Ramsay

———
Pădurar: forest warden.

RUNNING LIKE THE WIND

Now I see
what it means
to run like the wind.

From an entry
across the *bulevard*
a little lad – waif,
ragamuffin, tyke – face
wrapped in grey cloth,
races into the road
obliquely, straight toward me.

No-one in pursuit.
No hue and cry.
Not another soul in sight.

Over the tram lines
he skims.

The lights change.

Past
so close

the wind
brushes my hand.

THE UNCERTAINTY OF SPRING

Today we returned the geraniums
to the balcony with new cuttings,
and pots of chilli plants between.

Geraniums are uncool.
Chillies we designate hot.

In University Square two young
men spare each other
not a glance,

one in ironed
t-shirt laughing
into his phone,

the other in winter coat,
lugging a carrier bag
scuffed and bulging with files.

They say a young man
needs to 'come out of himself'.

A sycamore seedling
in the pot where
it fell last autumn

struggles
to shed
its helicopter casing.

CE SĂ FAC?

My customary short-cut:
by Everest fast-food,
past the (mostly) cheery
one-legged beggar,
toward Her Britannic Majesty's
Embassy through the rectangular
concrete arch under the flats –

where a boy aged
certainly less than he looks
sleeps on cardboard
under a green and white
tablecloth, one bare foot
aerating unwashed dreams.

Somn uşor
('sleep easy', 'sleep well' –
uşor meaning also 'light',
'gentle')...

As I pass by
uşor

a nerve is touched.
'Silver and gold
have I none...'

These days (*pardon,*
through the queue
for visas) I have only
a plastic square.
'But such as I have...'

So every day
wherever he lies
I pray 'in the name'.
And promise
what I can give is what I can do.

Better swing
crutched and cheerful
where no visa is required
than prevaricate in these inner courts.

The burden of the un-self-justifying
is 'easy',

their yoke
is 'light'.

James Ramsay

Ce să fac?: 'what can one do?', a general expression of resignation to an
overwhelming situation.

THE ENTERTAINER

Killing time before catching the overnight train from Budapest

Pleasure boats traverse
the open doorway
beneath floodlit Buda.
A battered grand piano
draped in amber velours
supports a brandy glass
primed with coins and a note.
The pianist hums, humming
modulates to song, capsicum
lips mouth '*Zigeuner!*'
to the German diners
at the only other occupied
table as padded shoulders
leap the length of the keyboard,
and the waitress wiping glasses
at the bar moves to the dance.

Pause for a smoke. 'Nationality?
British! Ah, then... the Beatles?
Elton John?' (With that dash of paprika.)
But my tastes are classical.
'Dvořák?' she tries. 'Chopin?'
Couples by the river kiss
to a waltz punched out like ragtime.

For the Dvořák the waiter
recommends a peach liqueur.

New customers arrive, the room
is crowded, I can no longer see
in a niche in the back wall,
inclining, all obsequiousness
and mockery, the three-foot-high
bright-glazed harlequin I had admired
when I had the place to myself.

Da capo to the *Zigeuner*
theme and time to head
for my sleeper to Bucharest.
The brandy glass clinks
with the last of my change.
But surely I would like a CD?
Inclining from the waist –
though lacking the lustre
of Herend porcelain –

I give the Tourist's Apology.

Read more books published
by Small Stations Press:

Karen Harrison, **A STUDY IN ENTROPY**

Entropy as a concept describes the
transformation or transition from a stable
to an unstable state. It characterizes any
thermodynamic system. This is the theme and structure of the
forty-seven poems in the collection *A Study in Entropy*. Most
represent accumulation or desire for extremity, followed by
destruction, expiry as an almost sacred gesture, like that of the
Danaids, at the end and the beginning always with the heavenly:
God, the Universe, the angels, the transcendent. The main topics
are death, pain, hope, faith, water. It is a journey through the Sacred
Mountain called life (in the process of writing the book the author
visited twenty places around the world, from Iceland to Kenya) and
incarnated deep in the heart. Karen Harrison's entropy, caused by
external circumstances, by the chaos of everyday life, by spiritual
and physical wounds, has its point of balance – survival, achieved
at the expense of courage and commitment. The book contains an
introduction by the Bulgarian poet Tsvetanka Elenkova.

ISBN 978-954-384-131-8

Jonathan Dunne, **SEVEN BRIEF LESSONS ON LANGUAGE**

Language is encoded. The words we use every day can tell us something about the meaning of human life, our purpose in this world, the divine being known as God, the creation of the world, the Fall, the economy, the environment... Once our eyes are opened at birth or soon after, we think that we see, but we do not realize that there is another level to reality, a spiritual dimension, for which we need our *spiritual* eyes to be opened. When this happens, when we believe in God and participate in the sacraments of the Church, we begin to perceive God all around us, in everyday objects such as trees, rocks, nature. These other realities, hitherto unseen, are called 'logoi' in Greek – fragments of the Word. They are also present in language. Apart from the meaning we give them, words contain their own meaning. They can be read in reverse, the letters can be rearranged or changed according to the rules of phonetics, their order in the alphabet, their appearance. The rules that must be followed to find connections between words and uncover their deeper meaning are always the same. *Seven Brief Lessons on Language* aims to give the reader a simple, but in-depth view of the spiritual side to language. Its title and format are adapted from Carlo Rovelli's book *Seven Brief Lessons on Physics*, but the content is entirely different. Each chapter can be read in a single sitting. Put together, these seven lessons (and a short postscript) will open the reader's eyes to a reality they never knew existed.

ISBN 978-954-384-129-5

Carys Evans-Corrales, TALKING GIRL

In this extraordinary account, Carys Evans-Corrales takes the reader on a cultural rollercoaster ride. As a child growing up in the Singapore, Malaysia and Jamaica of the 1950s and 1960s, the author came into contact with a host of languages and cultural influences, ranging from the Hainanese she spoke as a toddler to the Welsh counting song and English nursery rhymes she was taught by her mother to the Mandarin songs of Chinese children. In Kuala Lumpur, she came into contact with Malay, whose idioms delighted her, and in Kingston, Jamaica, with Jamaican patois, where she was shocked by the racially charged atmosphere. In Jamaica, she was introduced to Spanish, which conditioned her next move – to study Linguistics at York University in the UK, specializing in Spanish. This, in turn, led to a year abroad in Seville, where the author played the role of Andalusian *novia*, and, after completing her undergraduate degree, to a year of research in Salamanca. During this year, she was offered a job at the university in Santiago de Compostela, where she went in 1974, just as the Franco years were coming to an end and Galicia was recovering its language and identity. But it was in a move to America, in 1985, that the author finally acquired her own identity and laid the ghosts of her past to rest. The account of these years is littered with anecdotes about local people, school friends, linguistic conundrums and political backdrops, and offers a sweeping view of the second half of the twentieth century lived out on three continents.

ISBN 978-954-384-025-0

For an up-to-date list of our publications, please visit
www.smallstations.com

Index of Titles